SECOND VIOLIN

BOOK III · VIOLIN PART

GW00480842

THE ASSOCIATED BOARD OF
THE ROYAL SCHOOLS OF MUSIC

Preludio
from Sonata in E minor

Edited by
HOWARD FERGUSON

CORELLI, Op.5 No.8

The original consisted only of the violin part and figured-bass.

© 1972 by The Associated Board of the Royal Schools of Music

Allemanda
from Sonata in B flat

Arranged by
WILLIAM COLE

VIVALDI, Op.5 No.3

Allegro
from Sonata in A

HANDEL, Op. 1 No. 3

Corrente
from Sonata in G

Edited by
HOWARD FERGUSON

SENAILLÉ

The original consisted of the violin part and figured-bass.

AB 1806

Sarabande
from Sonata in D

LECLAIR, Op.9 No.3

Nocturne

BURGMÜLLER

This Nocturne is No. 1 of three Nocturnes 'Les Murmures du Rhone'.

Albumleaf

YORK BOWEN

Allegretto grazioso

Pastorale

HERBERT KINSEY

Petit Berger

PEGGY COCHRANE

Gipsy Dance

A. C. MACKENZIE

SECOND VIOLIN

Rachel Nichols

BOOK III

THE ASSOCIATED BOARD OF
THE ROYAL SCHOOLS OF MUSIC

Preludio
from Sonata in E minor

Edited by
HOWARD FERGUSON

CORELLI, Op.5 No.8

The original consisted only of the violin part and figured-bass.

Allemanda
from Sonata in B flat

Edited by
WILLIAM COLE

VIVALDI, Op.5 No.3

Allegro
from Sonata in A

HANDEL, Op.1 No.3

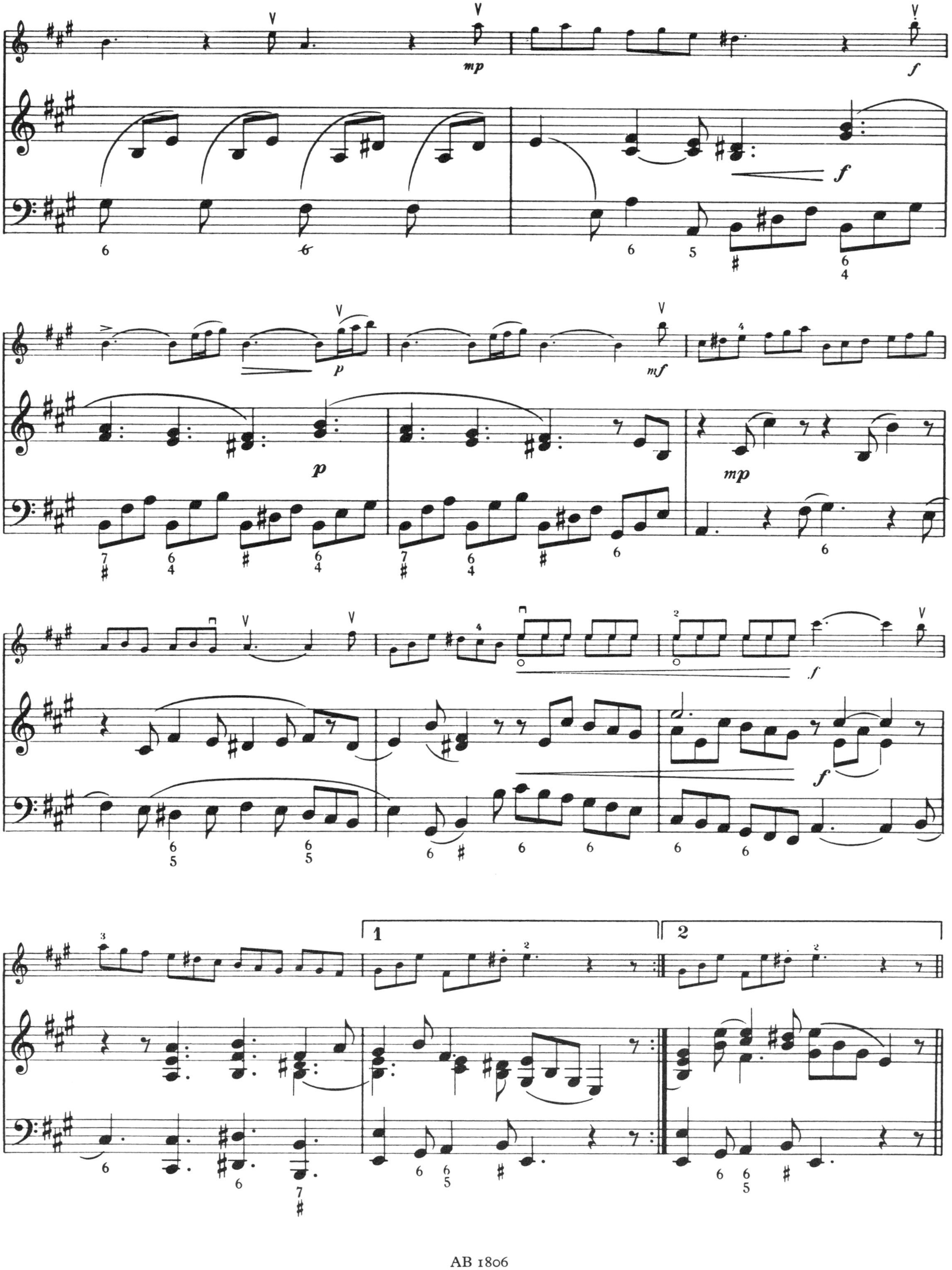

mp
f
p
mf
mp
f
1
2

Corrente
from Sonata in G

Edited by
HOWARD FERGUSON

SENAILLÉ

The original consisted of the violin part and figured-bass.

© 1972 by The Associated Board of the Royal Schools of Music

AB 1806

Sarabande
from Sonata in D

LECLAIR, Op.9 No.3

Nocturne

BURGMÜLLER

This Nocturne is No. 1 of three Nocturnes 'Les Murmures du Rhone'.

18

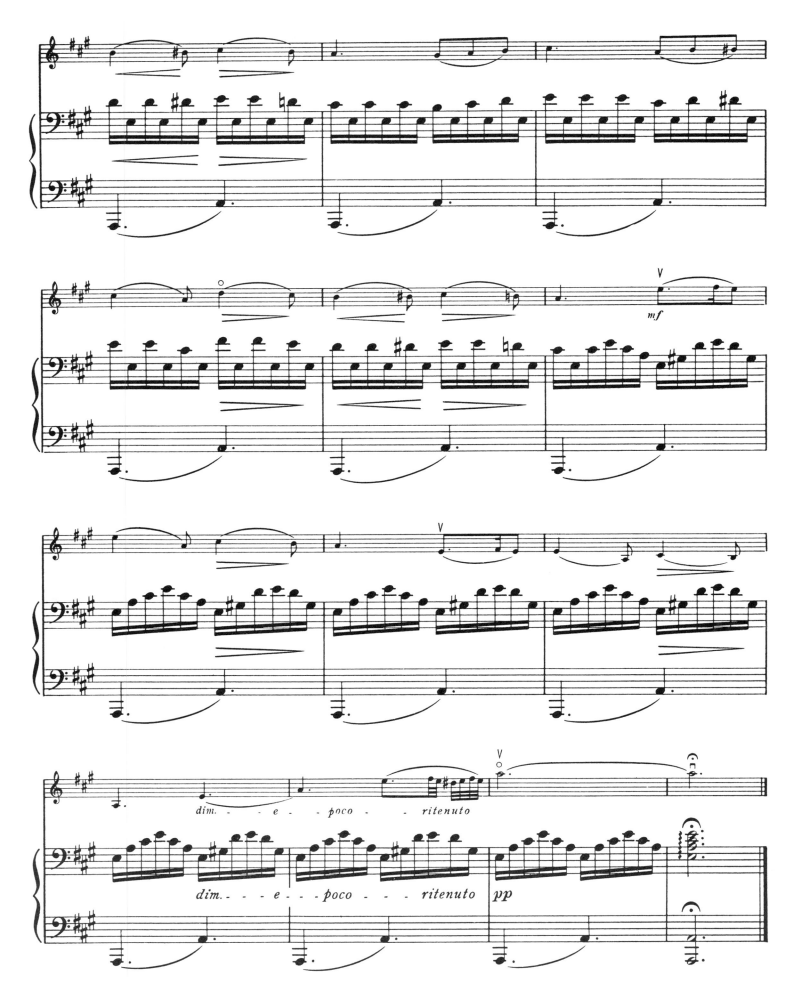

Albumleaf

YORK BOWEN

Pastorale

HERBERT KINSEY

Petit Berger

PEGGY COCHRANE

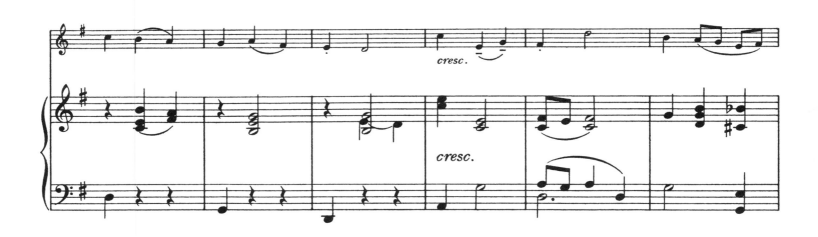

Gipsy Dance

A. C. MACKENZIE

Printed in England by Caligraving Limited Thetford Norfolk

AB 1806